The Ultimate Dark Web, Anonymity, Privacy & Security

SADANAND PUJARI

Published by SADANAND PUJARI, 2023.

Table of Contents

Copyright

The Ultimate Dark Web, Anonymity, Privacy & Security

First Edition: Dec 2023

Book Design by **SADANAND PUJARI**

About

Welcome to the ultimate dark net, privacy, anonymity and security Book. With no prior knowledge required this Book will take you from a beginner to advanced in all of these topics; teaching you how to properly and securely discover data and websites on both the dark web and clear web, access hidden (onion) services, communicate privately and anonymously using instant messages and email, manually use end-to-end encryption to protect your privacy and make it impossible to read even if it gets intercepted, sign and verify files, share files anonymously, transfer funds anonymously using crypto currencies such as Bitcoin and Monero and much more!

You'll also learn how to do all of this in a secure manner making it very difficult for hackers or other entities to hack you or de-anonymise you, and even if you get hacked these entities won't be able to easily control your system or de-anonymise you.

This Book is highly practical but won't neglect the theory, first you'll understand the inner-workings of each topic and each technique covered, then you'll learn how to apply it in real-life scenarios ultimately teaching you how to use the darknet and the clear net in a more private, more anonymous and more secure manner, so by the end of the Book you'll be able to combine the skills you learned and use them in any situation that requires more privacy, more anonymity or more security.

Introduction

All right so guys and welcome once again to another of my Books. Before we start I'd like to thank you all for joining my class. It's really appreciated and I hope that at the end of this Book you will be able to understand all the information that has been transmitted in the schools. So let's start, this Book will be really how to help you use a tour of the tour browser and how to navigate on the deep web on a daily basis.

If you need that you can navigate there on a daily basis. Um what will be the content of the Book. So at first we are going to see what the deep web is. You cannot talk in depth. What is it? How it works what it's part of the deep web. After that we're gonna see what's the difference between the deep web and the dark web. So it's not the same thing we're going to see what's the difference. What are the major differences between both of those things?

How the deep web can be used for legal purposes. Because yeah the deep web is not only illegal stuff. So you're gonna learn this and learn how you can use the deep web in your everyday life. I think that we're gonna talk about the deep web myths so what's true what's not true. Uh we're gonna talk about some of them. What though. Which one is true? Which one are false we also when when all this is done this will be the first Terry to go part of the Book. Then we're gonna start. We are gonna start to be more practical. So we're gonna have an introduction to the tour we're gonna talk about the tour brochure.

Yes you know a lot of other browsers to navigate anonymously but for this Book we're going to talk about the work we're going to talk about all the tour security and everything that is around the tour security and how the tour security works and everything that is around it how you can navigate the in a secure way. Well you store in a secure way. After that I'm gonna talk about the concept of anonymity. Let's talk about Anonymous. We get to you. I will present you with different alternatives that you can have to talk about. I will give you some well some hints on how to use them and everything. But we are not going to go in depth about them.

You will just learn that they exist and that we are not going to use them. Practically after that we're gonna begin our journey. And here we are going to navigate that to the Deep Web. So I'm going out in style to meet you guys. And we are going to set everything up when this is done. We are gonna visit some deep web web sites that have ten Websites that you guys want. Well we will visit. We will look forward to it. Those are interesting Websites and it's well those are Web sites that are 100 percent legal so you will be able to visit them and just look at what it looks like. Um when it's all done we're going to see how we can make purchases on the deep web because. Yeah it's not like on the normal web where you can just put on your credit card and that's it. It's a bit different.

We'll talk about crypto currency also because well crypto currency is the currency that is used on the Deep Web to buy stuff. We're gonna talk about this. We're going to talk about the purchase itself when it's well after this part you should know how to get to the Deep Web. Very basically. After that we are going to talk about all the dangers that can happen on the deep web slash Darknet. More from the dark web than on the deep web. What are those dangers? And we're going to talk in-depth about each and every danger that is here.

It's not like in the movies and everything where creepy stuff happens and we're going to talk about the real dangers that can happen. After that I'm going to give you some tips to stay safe and what to do and what not to do to stay safe on the Deep Web. And when this will be done well we'll have a small summary where we're going to talk about the whole Book. After that you should have all the knowledge that you need to be able to navigate through that. So the objective disBook is really to initiate you guys to the Deep Web. I'm not going to talk about some fancy advanced techniques to navigate 100 percent anonymously by using virtual machines and one hundred other things we are going to do.

My goal is really to initiate you towards the Tour rather than initiate you to the Deep Web. So this way you know what's this and how it works. What's a myth and what's true and what's false. What you will have to expect from going to this side of the Internet and then we are gonna go to break this fear that you have guys off the deep web when we were gonna go together at the site of the Internet and you will see how it really is and how everything works on this site.

Also the objective of this Book is really to finish well as I said this really initiates you and also to initiate you to the concept of anonymity and how you can navigate anonymously what you will be able to complete by the end of this Book. Well by the end of this Book you guys should be able to by yourself be able to download to a browser and use it 100 percent in a safe way. You will be able to navigate on all people it will deploy with Web sites on.

You will be able to find good deep web sites and navigate through them without fearing that you're going to get on some weird Web site somewhere on the dark web. So really at the end of this Book you will be able to buy yourself to navigate on the dark web you will not be you will not need a coach. Also you will be able to meet by yourself purchases by your own cryptocurrency and from buying your own cryptocurrency you'll be able to buy your own goods on the deep web and you'll understand how all this works. So that's it for the introduction guys. And see you in our next class where we are going to talk more in depth. What is the deep web?

What Is The Deep Web

All right. So once again guys. And welcome back to our amazing Book about the complete introduction to the Deep Web. So in today's class we are going to talk about what is the deep web. So we are going to see what's the deep web and what's the difference between the deep web and the surface web. We are not going to talk about the dark web in this Book. But in the next class we are going to talk a bit more in-depth about the dark web. So let's start. All right. So maybe you saw a picture of an iceberg on Google somewhere that says that's.

Well you have four percent of the web. That is the surface web. And then you have the deep web that is like 94 96 percent of all web. Well this picture is a bit too wide because technically the deep web is just another part of the Internet. It's like hiding on the web. If you say it this way, why is it this way? Well it's very simple. The deep web includes all the pages that are not indexed by a search engine, for example by Google. So what does this make? Well this includes pages for example YouTube Facebook or any other Web site that is indexed by Google will be the surface web as I said or pages indexed or the surface web.

And then you have all the pages that are not indexed. So you have millions and billions and billions and billions of pages. And those pages are mostly boring stuff. For example it could be your bank account. It could be your e-mail. It could be pages will be basically all pages that are protected by password could be for example a Website that is under construction right now. So for example a Web site that is under construction will not be indexed by a search engine. And if it's not indexed by a search engine well this means that the Web site is not on the web yet. Well he's maybe on the web but he is not indexed. So it's part of the web and as soon as it gets indexed Well it's going to be part of the surface web. So you have those pages at first then you can have web searches.

Those pages are basically old pages of let's say during pages we can say what for example let's say you have Yahoo or Google. Well they have old versions of them that exist but they are just not indexed anymore. So those pages will be in the archives. You can access them by using some applications that exist to access older pages. But once again they are just not indexed anymore. And you have online content. So that's very simple. It's all the content on the web that has no backlinks. So let's say for example Web sites such as Quora where YouTube does Web sites have a lot of content and they have a lot of backlinks.

Basically it helps them with you but that's not the topic of our Book backlinks. Give your Web site visibility for example you do. You put a link on your Web site, let's say on YouTube and people will see this link as a feedback link. So Websites that have absolutely no backlinks and they just exist. They have maybe some content but they have no back lanes. They have nothing. Well those Web sites are very likely not indexed by search engines. And if they're not, they will be part of the deep web and as I mentioned before well the majority of the Internet is really on the deep web so what type of content can you find it can be found on the deep web. Once again we are not gonna.

We're not talking about the dark web. So the deep web as I said it could be any type of content possible and that is imaginable and that you don't need to really well you will for that the dark web you will need the specific software and everything before the deep web. Well it really depends. Um well as I mentioned before uh the type of content that you can find on the deep web will be mostly boring stuff. For example e-mails which are bank account statements and those speeches are usually protected by passwords and things that you can't really really connect with, so let's answer some questions about the deep web. So the first one is that the deep web is illegal.

Well not really. It's in itself not illegal. If we talk about the dark web or deep web or the web, both of them are not illegal in themselves because you can have a lot of very very interesting information right there that you can really find on the surface web. But once again it depends what you want to do with it. Some activities right there can be considered as illegal but once again the concept of the weather web is not illegal but all what. How dangerous. Well how dangerous is the deep web. Once again it's more boring than dangerous because it's just a huge amount of pages. So let's say imagine.

Well the normal web is the surface web is like let's say a small library while the deep web lets say it's a huge huge huge huge library. So it's mostly as I said boring stuff. So it's not dangerous but once again it's like if you're visiting a Website on the surface web that has let's say viruses viruses worm malware as well you are as exposed as if you visit a Website that has viruses or my wares on the Deep Web. But we are not going to talk really in-depth about all the dangers of the deep web because yes you have some dangers on the deep web that you're not necessarily have on the surface web because well the quality of pages and the content are different.

Well some of you have some other type of content on the deep web sometimes. But once again the most part of the deep web is like the surface web. It's really boring stuff. It's the deep web. Same as the dark web. Once again you know it's both of them are different. We are not gonna talk about it in this class, we are going to talk about it in our next class. And the last question that we are gonna suck is uh can Google search the deep web. Well since it's not indexed on the deep web since it's not. Well since the pages that are on the deep web are not indexed by Google. Well not really because Google is not.

It's not taking this page and those pages in consideration because the majority of them are well private or they don't want Google to index them and it's understandable for example an email service. Well they will not want Google to index for example pages that are supposed to be private. So those speeches are private and only strictly reserved to the person that owns an email. For example once again this is part of the deep web. Ok one last question. What kind of stuff you can buy on the deep slash dark web. You can absolutely buy anything. That's the thing, it's like a huge market.

Well you have a lot of marketplaces on the surface web. You have marketplaces such as Amazon where there are many different things on the Deep Web. Well you have other marketplaces you have normal like in places like Amazon but you have other types of marketplaces where you're gonna talk about it in our next classes. But once again all of this is really just for educational purposes. And just so you guys know that this exists. So that's it for this court guys. And see you all in our next class.

Difference Between The Deep Web And The Dark Web

All right. So once again hello. Yes and welcome back to our Quest about the complete introduction to the Deep Web. Well deep slash dark web face glass. We are gonna see the difference between both of those things. So what's the difference between the deep and the dark web? Uh you're gonna see us. Um the difference well there is a difference between the both of them as we mentioned.

As I mentioned before our last glass at the deep web is just a place where for example there is no indication from search engines what this means. This means that all heights and beaches can be considered as pages from the Deep Web. It's let's say one layer of protection but the Dark Web is a bit different. We're going to see why. So the Dark Web the way you can see it first of all it's well imagined the deep web. Right now the deep web has another layer of protection. So first of all to access the Dark Web or the so-called dark side of the Internet.

You need a special software by special software we are talking about software like Tor for example which is the most use software in the software in the most popular software to access to the spirit of the Internet. Once again it's one and you have a lot of other software that you can use not that much but you have some other software that can do the job like Tor in this class. We are really going to focus more on the tour. We're going to work with it. We're going to work with another software but we will principally be working with our so you will need special software to access those pages because those speeches are not dot.com pages. They are dot onion pages. As you can see in the powerpoint.

Why is it like this? Well it's simple, you just can't access them on a regular search engine. For example if you take a page from the dark web you can connect the speech to a search engine. If you take a page from the Deep Web for example you want to access someone else's Netflix account. Well if you think that you are all of the person's Netflix account you're going to write it down and you will be on the main page of Netflix because you have to enter the user name and the password to get access to the beach of the person speech on Netflix will be part of the Deep Web. But next Netflix as a whole like itself will be part of this service. What is the dark web? As I said it's really a part of the Internet that is hidden.

Once again it's not as people say a place where a lot of bad stuff happens. Yes you have this part of the Internet. But once again it can be used very legally, very legally and for a good purpose. So the third thing is that most beaches are very hard to find. Why? Because you don't really have search engines as you have on the regular internet. The way you will search on the deep web is. Well on the dark web is that you will really need to have the specific you are out of the place that you want to visit. It's very very important. And you can just play around and click anywhere because well it's not a good thing to do.

Used principally on the dark web it's a better thing to do. So do you. You visit the Web. Well you need to have a specific you or else you can just click on some random beaches or just do your research as you do on the regular web. Because as I said the majority of things that are out there are not boring and not very very good. But think about the things people say. But you have some part of the Internet that is a bit more dark.

Let's see it this way. What type of information you can find there. Other cryptic documents you can have more cryptic documents once again you need to have access to the Web site you need to find the places where those documents are. Sometimes it can be really really good. Important documents you have legal anonymous marketplaces. So yes you have marketplaces not as big. Well we are smaller than Amazon but those types of market places you can find honestly anything on the deep web you can find people who are selling TV people who are selling cell phones people who are selling all of legal stuff. And once again I don't know why they sell it there, maybe it works for them. Well I don't judge it's their business. So yeah you have a legal anonymous marketplace.

And the difference once again another difference between the well the surface web slash and part of the deep web and the Dark Web is that well on the dark web everything is anonymous. So it's not on the point but everything on the Deep Web. Well on the Dark Web is let's say Anonymous because the software that you were gonna use which is stored well it helps you stay anonymous. Yes it's not 100 percent anonymity because yes you can be tracked and all this stuff. But once again the purpose of the deep web is really anonymous. Well going on the Internet anonymously we're going to talk about it in our future classes about the concept of anonymity.

OK so just for you to understand. Yes. You have a leak complete legal anonymous marketplace.

Also what you have also is a complete illegal. Huge illegal network. So when I say huge legal network you have absolutely everything you can have it dangle from drugs guns to let's say for all the credit cards. Well a lot of bad things can be there because once again those. This part of the Internet there. There is no law there. Everyone is anonymous. So people do pretty much what they want. This is why there is a lot of mystery around the deep well of the dark web there. Well more dark web. There is a huge mystery around this thing because people think it's just evil and only that but people will be there. But once again no it's a small part of the Internet. It's not like the whole deep web like the deep web.

Let's say it's 94 percent of the Internet but the dark web and the bad things of the dark web are just a tiny percentage of it not as people say. But yeah you can have very very bad stuff. For example, an illegal network can have really bad stuff and can have racist content. You can have some very bad Websites. So yeah. So that's it for this cause. Right now you know the difference between the deep web and the dark web. Um uh besides that I have nothing to say for this glass.

So see in our next glass where we are gonna go a little bit more in the deep web and see how this will be, how this could be used for legal purposes and what exactly you can do. Well what legal things you can find on the Deep Web that could help you in your everyday life. So see you in our next clicks. Guys thanks for reading.

How The Deep Web Could Be Used For Legal And Good Purposes

All right. We'll see you. Hello guys and welcome to another of our classes about the complete introduction to the Web. So in this class we are going to talk about how the deep dark web could be used for legal purposes. Yes. Since I mentioned in our last class the deep web slash dark with the deep slash Dark Web is not only bad things. The deep deep web itself.

Well it could be a lot of interesting things just well not indexed by Google and the dark web. Well there too you have a lot of interesting things. But once again you have a lot of bad things. So let's see how we can do this. Two forms of web can be used for legal purposes. All right. So the first thing is it provides people anonymously. So the main goal of the tour and all this concept of deep slash dark web and everything well everything behind this is really becoming anonymous. So people want to be able to have some privacy when they're browsing. And with these browsers for example if you go on Chrome or Internet Explorer or whatever everything you do that the more the more small movement you do well you are being tracked by different cookies and that will what's happening is that you are constantly well be huge theorems the firms in this world are constantly getting information from you.

So this way they give you a lot of ads and you buy their products and all this kind of stuff but with the deep web it's completely different. You are 100 percent anonymous. No one tracks you. You are let's say free to do whatever you want so that's an amazing thing. It provides anonymity. Yeah Of course a lot of people why people are so scared of the deep web or the Dark Web is because well they're used to safe places for example. Well Google it's what Google or any other browser internet or Mozilla. Well they are safe places and Websites that you can find there are safe Websites and usually you don't expect to see like stuff that you can see on the web because people will not post this kind of stuff because they and they can get tracked but on the deep slash their web it's different since everyone is anonymous.

Well people post any kind of stuff. This is why you can have access to. Well you can have access to that stuff but you can also have access to amazing stuff. And what I'm talking about is amazing stuff. We're gonna talk about it. And our last point. Also it could be good in any kind of information. The second thing it gives access to is well censored content to people from some countries. What does it mean? Well what I'm trying to say by this is let's say for example you have countries that have some Web sites that are censored that you can't access for example in some countries in the world you can't access Facebook where you can access YouTube. So people who are living in those countries are living well or experiencing massive censorship that prevents you from accessing some websites. So what's happening is that they don't see the Internet as we see it in other countries, for example in Canada. Yes.

In The United States we have access to content that people in China will not necessarily have access to because the Internet is a control. So the the deep web well the deep web the browser that that well that controls that gives you access that a deep web will give you access to all the data and you will be able to well get access to a lot of content that is censored by governments and you will be able to read this content which is an amazing thing. And once again it brings us to the point that a lot of information is available on the deep web since it's around ninety five well from 140 96 percent of the whole Internet. You have amazing amazing content right there. And for the censors. For the censorship part even this for example people were living in a certain country. Well they will be able to see the world differently.

Let's say the government tries to not oppress you but the government tries. Usually in most people's well the government controls media the government controls everything and by accessing the deep web tools people will be able to see the world like they will see the world differently. They will not only see what their government or media is telling them to see. Let's think it has what it brings us to our last point which is it has a lot of massive information. So what I'm trying to say by massive information well first of all you have all those Websites that people can't access will be able to access by going to the Web. And you have huge libraries, you have books, all kinds Of courses you have.

Well when you get the deep web you have one thing that is the tour library I'm not mistaken. And well you will be able to have access to a huge database Of courses that you can read. So it's a lot of information. Also since it's like the biggest part of the Internet. Well by getting access to the deep web slash dark web you'll be able to get access to a lot of beautiful information from different countries. Well different people only just do the concept of having access to what other people say you are the point of view of some people on some things or some situations. Well it's really a beautiful thing because once again people are anonymous and people do not retain their sight of seeing the real things like what they really think.

And this way you can once again see really beautiful things but you can also see very bad things. So this is why it's very important to know where exactly you will look to find your information because as I said you don't have censorship on the Deep Web. Well the large dark web since everyone is anonymous so no censorship means people can say and do whatever they want without necessarily getting tracked. Even if some people are getting tracked, this is the concept of the deep dark web. It's really to give you the Mahdi and give you the power to say things or do things without being censored. So it could be a good thing. A very very good thing but it can also be a bad thing.

So this is why you have to filter where you tried to find out your information. So those are the things that you can do spirit of things. There are ways for you to use the deep web legally, as I said, to find out information. Once again it could be scientific information it can be information about a lot of different stuff about history about countries. Personally I really love that tour library because you have books about absolutely everything. So yes this is personally why I use the deep web very very often because as I said you have a lot of beautiful information and you just have to know where to find this information and how to filter all this information because yes sometimes you can find very bad things.

But once again if you filter right, if you filter the information directly everything's fine. You're right. So those are the three things that for me I consider can be considered as well you will use the web for legal purposes anonymously to give access to censored content for it's for countries that live in censorship. So those people will have access to the whole Internet as a whole and will give access to a lot of information that is not necessarily on the surface web but that can be very present on the deep slash dark web. So that's it for this cause guys. And see you in our next class where we talk about myths about the dark slacks, the deep slash.

Deep Web / Dark Web Myths

It's only been a few years. Welcome back. That is Of course our Book, the complete introduction to the dark web. So Of course we are going to talk about the principal myths and legends that are around the Deep Web. I'll give you some examples and a disBook that you will see on the point and I'll give some other examples as well. So let's start, the first myth is that the Dark Web is huge.

Once again I'm not talking about the deep web. I'm talking about the dark web itself. So the deep web is as I said something around ninety four point eighty six percent of the whole Internet. The Dark Web, the dark web himself. Well it's not that big compared to all this. It's only something about something around 500000 Web sites. So once again it's very very small compared to the deep web as a whole. So once again when we talk about the Dark Web it is all the things that are hiding beside the network and all the things that you need.

Well another you need special software is to get access to so once again it's not that huge. If we compare it to the surface web or if we compare it to the whole deep web as a whole. So once again that's from sources that you can find on. Well if you do your research the sources mentioned that it's not that big right. So the same thing. The Dark Web is illegal. So and so now you know that the dark web has some very bad things in them. But once again it's not illegal in itself. Getting access to the web is like getting on the dark web and stealing this software and getting on. I don't know that any type of Website on a dark web is not illegal. It's what you're doing after that.

For example you just get on the dark web and play around and visit. Well it's not illegal but if you try to buy it let's say weapons. Well if that's where it becomes legal. So the dirt as I said dark web has itself is not illegal. It's even legal to go on it because. Well as I said, my best classes can have very interesting information there. And well you can use it for a lot of educational stuff. Well educational purposes as I said you have a lot Of courses you have a lot of points of view on a lot of different things. It's really an amazing place. If you know how to use it because if you don't know how to use it well it can be very bad.

Third thing is that the Dark Web is completely anonymous. So yes by using the software is associated with getting access to the deep slash dark web you are supposed to be anonymous but once again it depends what you're doing online. So there are a lot of people that are attracted by the dark web and not all, not all of those people are there for the right reasons. So you can have hackers. That's a huge place for hackers and yes you can get attacked. Yes. Depends what you're doing. There is some kind of stuff that if you do well you can get in trouble with law enforcement, for example getting attacked by other people on the dark web because once again if you are there just learn things and just to read books and to get information.

Well it's not a big deal. But once again if you trade it it's it's and then it's anonymous until someone wants to track you. For example if the law wants to track you because you've done something illegal. Well then it's not going to be an honest man anonymous anymore because they have the budget to find you so yeah it's anonymous but just a certain point. It's not completely anonymous. No, there is nothing on the Internet that is 100 percent anonymous.

Dark Web is only used for crimes. So until now I think you know my point of view about the dark web if you know how to use it the right way. Well it's not a bad thing. Once again as I said you can find beautiful information. You can find books that you can't necessarily find in libraries or books that are very very hard to find on Amazon. You can find PDX of those books. You can find really quality information there as well as the forums on a lot of different topics which can be political and financial about governments. There is no censorship. So once again it's not only for crimes it's for people like you and me who just want to learn new things.

Yes you have criminals on the dark web but you have even more criminals on the surface web. Why is it like this? Because on the surface web there are a lot more people. So if we talk about cyber criminality trust me the hackers will be more present on this on the surface web on the deep web because on the Dark Web site because the dark web doesn't have a lot of traffic compared to the surface web that's why hackers tend to attack more surface web web sites than dark web web sites because it's harder to attack those Websites that are on the dark web because once again there is not that much traffic and everyone's using the Twitter network and it's way more harder to reach those people than to reach people on surface web where the information is way more accessible.

If we talk about crimes like not cyber crimes or real crimes. Well that's the exact same thing. Criminal criminal activities happen more on the surface web than they happen in the dark on the deep slash dark web. Because once again there are way more people on the surface web than on the dark deep slash dark web. So yeah that's where the crimes and once again as I told you before the deep dark web can be used for a lot of good stuff for a lot of good purposes. So for me it's not a place for crimes and for a lot of people who know how to use them. It's not a place of crimes. It can be once again a good place for information.

It's very hard actually there. But now it's very easy to get access to the Dark Web. What's hard? It's navigating the Dark Web right with filing. Well, finding Web sites or links to different Web sites it's very easy. But once again you don't want to get on the Web sites where you have viruses and your computer gets attacked or shut down because once again it's not a crime. It's not a place on the programs. But once again if you click on the wrong link well you can get on the Web sites that you don't really want to get on. This is why it's not hard to access it but using it the right way. Well it's a bit harder. It's gonna take you a bit of time to find places where you can find the things that you're looking for. For example, you want to find information.

I don't know about let's say political regime of a certain country. Well, do you have specialized Websites there? Let's say you want to find a book about I don't know the sea. Well you have places on the deep web where you can find this book where books related to your subject. You have places where you have a lot of knowledge. So once again it's not hard to access the dark web but it's harder to know how to navigate the right way. True. Well the right way through the good dark web. So you don't really need to be an expert to get access to this Web site. So that's that for all the myths that are around the dark web.

And then once again it's very important for you guys to not believe all the creepy pasta that you can see on YouTube or any other platform about the deep dark web because a lot of those people are saying well we're seeing a lot of things about deep those dark web is that they are never been there or they've been there for like 30 seconds each and they just leave. Leap because once again it's if you know how to use it the right way. Well it's not. It's more boring. It's like the normal internet but just Web sites are less and less let's say flash you are less attractive. That's the only thing. But besides that if you know how to use it.

Well it's a really great place to learn new things. And well most of all learn new things and read new books. So let's try this Book guys. And I hope you enjoyed it. See you in our next class where we are going to talk about the software that we can use to get access to the deep web.

Introduction to TOR

All right. Once again Hello guys. Welcome back. Of course the deep web is the complete introduction so into this class we are going to have an introduction to tour. Um why tour. It Is very simple to access the deep web. I. Well the dark web. I've told you that you will have to use software , so the software that we are gonna use today is the most popular software that exists on the market. This software is stored. So this is why we are gonna talk about it. So first of all what store. Tourism. No. Nope source project.

This means everyone can contribute to the project. The main goal of this project is really to promote anonymous navigation and then turn it this way people can have access to information that they want without having to reveal to everyone who they are. So it really helps with how the browser works. It's very simple. The tour browser works on your network. So when you see an onion what do you see? Usually an onion has a lot of layers. So that's exactly the same thing. When we talk about Tor you have Tor and let's say for example you use another web browser because your store is a web browser first. So let's say you use for example Google Chrome when you use Google Chrome and for example you want to get access to Google.

What's going to happen is that Google Chrome is going to send a request to Google server and the request will come back and give you access to Google with the two browsers. The request is gonna go so you will send a request from your computer but the request will go for example to the server where a computer is in another country and then another country and then another country and then finally go back to Google. So what just happened is that tourists sent it. Well if you send a request by a lot of computers this way does find the person who received that request. It's Google that received the request and the request will do. Once again the whole journey back to you. So why is this done? It's very simple it's because it's a good way for not getting track at least on a basic level because well the request passes to a lot of computer slash servers and this way people well people are making research on the Internet and way more harder to track than people who use for example Chrome or Mozilla where internet or just a simple VPN.

So if you ask a few questions that people ask, for example to hide my IP address yes or by passing to different computers, slash servers will hide your IP address. And that's one of the main goals of this software is really to help you stay anonymous online and by hiding your IP address is one way for you to stay anonymous online because no one will know where you are and from where you're browsing. Um yes Tor is a browser for people we're asking. So it's the same thing as Mozilla Firefox or Chrome or whatever. The only difference between this web browser and the other ones is that this one is focused on really staying anonymous. Is it free?

Yes, storage is completely free. As I said, an open source project. So it's completely free to get access to it. And no it's not illegal to use the store for. We're asking the deep web once again that it's not illegal so the software that is around getting access to this well to the site of the internet is also not illegal. Once again. Well why the browser was born one of them and then one of the main reasons why that web browser was born is really to help answer in need of anonymity when browsing online. So a lot of people are web browsing online and want to stay anonymous. And it's really really hard to be anonymous , especially online.

Because when you're browsing well even with Tor if someone wants to track you down there are ways to track it down. So with other browsers, it's very simple to track someone's down. This is why the web browser was born. Because it's really to help people stay anonymous online without having everyone know what they do. Exactly. So that's why the browser existed. And as I mentioned the main goal of the tour browser. Well it's very simple. It's getting people helping people stay anonymous, especially online. So that's the main goal of the door buzzer. The browser itself. Well the tour project began in 1980 1990 and it was fully developed around 2006 if I'm not mistaken the first version came out in 2002.

Well the initial release but. Yeah. So the project itself has something really beautiful behind it. Because as I said it's really to help people stay anonymous because as we know in today's society everyone's tracking everyone. So our project is really helpful for this. And yet besides that the tor browser as I said is really to help anonymity. So right now we have the same kind of idea about what store to work in if it's legal or illegal. And so as I said it's nothing strange, it's nothing that scares me that a web browser is just another browser like the other ones.

Well as any other browser the only difference between this browser and others is really that it's focused on staying anonymous and helping the person that uses it stay completely anonymous online. So that's the furthest Book gays can see in our next guest where we are going to talk about the security behind tor.

TOR Security

All right. Hello guys. Welcome back to another of our Books about the complete introduction to the deep web. Since this class we are going to talk about toy security and how to use Tor safely. So let's start. So what is thought of stands for The Onion Router. It comes well this is a web browser as we use as we talked about it. Now the last test. And gives the bot the possibility to people who use it to stay anonymous online and to get access to the Deep Web.

But is it safe to use? Well yes not normally it's safe to use. But you have to take some safety measures. Once again um Tor is not something that prevents you from getting viruses or mail malware or whatever to wear what I'm talking about safely. I'm talking from an anonymous point of view. So if you want to be anonymous or if you want to be let's say under a little when you are going on the Internet yes it does a pretty much good job it's not a 100 percent because no web browser can guarantee you 100 percent anonymity. But once again it does a pretty good job. So for dying, so for that encryption.

So how to protect your anonymity. As we mentioned last class. Well it uses an onion the way it works. It works like an onion. So it will start at your starting point and then let's say for example you want to go to Google. Well it's going to pass to the different let's say computers. It's like an onion when you take off layers from an onion when there are a lot of layers. It's really hard to get. First the let's say layer or first user who for example wanted to get access to Google which in this case is you because you are connected to Tor and you want to access a certain Web site. So let's see this. So for the data encryption part Well it's very very very it's it's very it's very but it's pretty much good. And yes. So it works pretty well.

Once again Tor doesn't prevent everything from end to end. So. Well from one bird to the other let's say from your site to the Web site you want to connect to and you will have to be careful because once again there are people who are able to track you if you do some bad things on the Deep Web. Um, so how do they say the first thing? Well, same thing. I mean you have to be careful with some plugins so when you're connected to the tower browser you don't want to download a lot of plugins that you can find on the Internet or on YouTube videos. Why? Because Tor is already completed. So when you download the program it's already completed. And if you download plugins well it can interfere with the job that is already done by the browser it itself works pretty well. So you don't have to add a lot of plugins to make it work better. It can.

It has more chances to put you at risk than to help you with anything. Because none of those plugins is guaranteed to be secure. That's the thing with all the plugins that you download to do it. Next thing is when you're navigating on the deep web and you want to be 100 percent sure that you're anonymous. I personally suggest you close all the apps that are connected to the Internet on your computer. So that's my suggestion. I personally do it. Um why. It's because well people say that they're what people say. There are ways that people can track you if you leave those apps open so it's just a tip that I personally use.

I don't leave the apps open on my computer when I'm navigating on let's say the deep web or when I'm connecting to the TOR browser so that I'm not a safety tip that I can give you. If you ever navigate on that web browser. Um. Next thing when you will be connected to a browser the Tor window will. It's gonna. Well it's gonna be a certain size so don't maximize the size of this window. Why? Because by maximizing the size of your window you are putting yourself at risk that you can get tracked or your anonymous city will decrease is when you will. Well where we will be at the point where we've got a download Tor you will see this morning when that web browser will be downloaded.

You will see the warning that you are not secure when your window is maximized or Max um and so this is why. That's another safety tip that I can give you. Um don't maximize your tour browser window leave it as it is. You will see the size of it is not that small so you'll be able to navigate comfortably from your computer on your browser without having to maximize it. Um next thing: Never ever ever download documents on the deep web or slash. I mean dark web Why. You know what's in the documents. You don't know how many viruses you can download, especially if you go on a streaming website and you want to download movies on the dark web.

Well it's a very bad idea to download movies there because there is more chances that you download some virus or some malware that will connect to your computer and steal all your data that you download only because all you all those Websites in the surface web are filled with ads and with viruses. So on the deep web it's even worse. You have even more chances to get a virus through your computer so never download no data. Never. If you receive an email on your well on your tour under a door on your Deep Web message service do not. Well you can open it but if you receive for example attachments to ask you to download something.

Well don't download it on the surface web. When you receive an email of something as someone who you don't know asking you to download something. Well the best thing to do is not think about it. Well it's the same thing on the Deep Web. Well don't do it because you'll see you're gonna get yourself in a lot of trouble especially if you don't have the intent of it. And antivirus or if you're not using a virtual machine. And in this Book we are not talking about connecting your finger well toward our virtual machine but I talk about tables but it's a bit different. But yeah I.

Let me just give you a quick. Well, virtual machines. If you connect through toward the virtual machine it's a bit different because you will be able to. Well if you catch that you say the viruses will only affect the virtual machine and will not affect your computer. Once again in this Book we are only talking about getting connected to the deep web, not using a lot of stuff to be 100 percent anonymous. Yeah. You said that. Don't play around with the darknet when you are on the darknet. You need it. Well what I suggest to you personally is you will have to. You will need to have a list of Websites you want to visit.

Let's say for example you want to visit this Web site or this Web site. Well you know where you're going you know exactly where you are. What exactly you want to visit. And if you need to do some research as well. Make them on the clear net or the surface web or. Well you can go on certain forums that can help you with this. But don't start looking around and clicking on all links that you can find on the deep web because there are more chances that go on an unwanted Web site than anything else. So once again be very very safe on this path. So you will need to have a clear Website where you want to go if not what Matrix researches on the surface web for the links and then only after that can you trade those links on the deep web. So let me summarize once again that our encryption for the well for the safety it's pretty much good.

So it works very well the right way. So be very careful with the plugins that you can download for the web browser that doubled nothing from the front when you visited the deep web. Nothing, nothing, never closed our apps when you were using Tor so don't forget about this all up close. Only the two hour window opens to maximize your door window. You're too wet to window because it can be tracked if it's maximized don't open and download documents or don't download no document.

No start downloading stuff because there can be viruses, malware or any kind of stuff you're not on the surface whether you're on the Dark Web so you have to be very careful it doesn't start to play around once again because you can get on Web sites that you don't want to get into. So that's where this Book goes. And then I see you all in our next class where we are gonna talk about the concept of anonymity.

The Concept Of Anonymity

All right I'll see you again soon. And welcome back to another of our classes Of course about the deep web. But in today's class we are going to talk about the concept of anonymity and tour alternatives. So when we are talking about the concept of me I really want to talk about why on anonymous why and this concept as an Oh. So let's start.

So the first question is why people want to be anonymous online so there can be a lot of reasons for this. First of all, people just want to be anonymous. People just don't like to be spied on or to feel that someone is watching them or whatever any kind of reason related to this second reason. For example, people are visiting sites that are censored in certain countries. So as I mentioned in my past classes there are countries in this world where you can't access some Websites. For example, some people can go on Facebook in some countries. So let's say they use the word browser.

Well they will be able to access Facebook or any other website for example in some countries. There are news websites that are banned. There are journalistic Websites that are banned. Well by using the Internet browser you will be able to access all those Websites just because you are. Well you will be able to access all those Websites so those are the major reasons why people want to be anonymous. Also if people want to write something let's say anonymously. Well they can do it on the deep web because. And by using that web browser does.

If they do it on the surface web. Well if living in a country where censorship is barely heard. Well they can be in a lot of trouble. So that's why the next thing. Is it possible to be anonymous online? So still we are well right now we are talking about the concept of anonymity. But is it possible to really be anonymous online? So personally I think not because the yes story gives you a certain anonymity and everything. And if you're using a VPN or any other thing that hides where you are. Yes you are anonymous until a certain point but if you are doing things if you're doing illegal things or any related stuff to this. Well there are a lot of chances that police or Internet Internet police will want to track you.

For example if you're a hacker and you're hiking or whatever. Well there's a lot of chances that the police on the entire internet will want to track you and they have a lot of budget. The difference between you and them is that they have a lot of budget. This means they have a lot of resources and they can even if you think you're anonymous well they're not really that anonymous. So yes there is a certain anonymity on the web but until a certain point once again if someone really wants to track you and has the resources well it's possible to track people even people who are using the web browser with. I don't know how many layers of protection there are. So yes it's possible to get on the mass online but you never can be 100 percent anonymous. That's the only thing.

Next question using it again versus tor browser. So basically the difference between a VPN and the tour browser is that a VPN will generally be faster and uh since they have their own servers. The main reason for that is because the chickens have their own servers to sort and Tor is a bit more much slower because trade depends on people who. Well people who are volunteers too well get the release of let's say you are going to Google. Well you need people to really want to go to Google. So they depend on volunteers. But the plans have servers VPN companies have servers all over the world. And that's why they are much much faster.

The only thing is that Tor well tor proves that it works and proves that it's something really very reliable and also tor it's free. So you don't have to pay for it. So personally I like Tor and honestly when you are going on the deep web only two for example let's say good read books or read some kind of news that are censored in some countries. Well with tor you will be okay. You don't need any fancy VPN or any other type of stuff. And don't try to use either VPN to tour or. Because usually as I mentioned my last class um talk comes with already built in features and the tour mentions it uh mentioned that when you install it. That it's not a good idea to just what when you install Tor to add other third party material to to third party plugins or add ons.

It's not a good idea because Tor already has his things and until now it works pretty well. So right now is there any alternative to Tor or not really. Once again that's a good question and that you have a lot of alternatives. But for me personally I know three of them that are that are very that works well the first one is that that works very well it's also a peer to peer platform. It helps. Well it has the same goal as that where uh it tries to well it tries to not promote censorship. It tries to decrease censorship in the world and the countries who are censoring some for example news, some data or some things. This platform, let's call it like this, is really against it. So if you're looking for something let's say Tor free Net there's like this.

The second well let's talk about the eye to be the second one to be is invisible Internet project. Once again that's another thing that is something like Tor. It's an anonymous network layer. Once again it has 55000 computers in the works a bit the same way as Tor so it's release. So for example you go on Google and it works exactly the same way. So there are releases that will pass by a lot of computers. So this way no one will be able to go back to you. Well it's gonna be hard to get back to you. And the last little thing. Well the last alternative to tour. Well it still is but it's not really a no turn alternative to tour because it works with Tor. And we are gonna. Well we are gonna download it.

Also we're gonna work a bit later in this class of hotels. It's very simple, it's a life system. And while his goal is also to preserve private Senate nominations anonymously, this system works directly with Tor and Tories integrated into Tales. So this way not only well it's a major advantage to have it because what's happening with tails is that you will have it on the US booking so you will be able to access the deep web anywhere. So let's say for example you're going. I don't know. In it, a car is in a coffee shop somewhere and you have your laptop for a. I don't know. You have a laptop or someone's laptop.

Well we can take you to have deals on it. Plug the laptop into the deep web, let's say read some news and we'll just unplug it and all the data will not be saved anywhere. It's going to be. Well it's gonna be raised so Thales is really really an amazing tool to use. And this is why we are gonna learn how it works. The best part about it is that everything that you guys are going to see in this Book while all the material that you guys are going to use in this Book includes tor work deals is completely free and it works very well it has been tested not only by me but by a lot of people on this planet. And also it's all legal and it works well once he works very very very well.

And for those who want to stay really anonymous or just navigate on the clear web anonymously. Well they're gonna see work. It's a very good way to do it. It's. It costs nothing. Yes. It's gonna be a bit slower because you will have to wait because as I explained toward the way it works it's a lot of people who. Well when you make a request to a server it's gonna really buy a lot of computers and this is one one of the reasons why it's a bit slow. If you have this if you have money and you want to pay for a VPN and you want to stay on the clear net well you can do it. But if your goal is to go on the Deep Web.

Well you're going to see Tor and tails. They will be your best friends. And in the next classes and even after this Book. So I think right now you understand what's the concept of anonymity and why people want to be anonymous. So what are some alternatives? Yes you have some other alternatives. But for me those three are pretty much very good. My favorite is tales that work directly with doors. So yes it's a thrill. But it also works with Tor so it's not really a toilet. It's like something that works with Tor. So that's it from this class guys and they're seeing our next class where we are gonna go on the field and we are gonna start working with Tor and we will install it.

Downloading TOR

All right so once again how little guys. And welcome back to our ninth class or Book about the deep web, the complete introduction since this class. We are going to download the tor browser on our computer and we'll set it up so this way you will be able to use it for. Well as a private well as the primary browser we're just as brother two brothers on the deepwater. So until now you know all the theories that you have to know to be able to download. Well to be able to navigate on the deep web. So let's start our journey right now.

So the first thing you want to do is open up your normal search engine. If you have Chrome will open up chrome then very simple you want when you're your search engine simply. Right. Don't talk when it's done. Well you can click on the first link. It should look like this. So it's going to be done now and you click on Download the browser when it's done. Very simply, simply choose your machine if you have a window. Download it for Windows Mac from Mac and X and Android. So you simply click on download and it's going to be downloaded on your machine. When it's done you should have a thing like this.

Well you should have this step that will appear which is start tor browser. You simply click on it. It's going to load. You'll see it's a bit slower than other browsers but it's because you have a lot of. Well you have at once on it that makes it more secure. So we'll see maybe the first time that you download it. It's gonna take a bit more time. All right. So here is our tor browser. So it should look something like this. So the first thing you want to do guys. Well the first thing we will see is how it is. So as you can see it's like the Mozilla web browser. Well the look is a bit the same. So let's look at the first thing I want to look for is what are the add ons as you can see you have already two add ons on your browser.

The first one is H2. Yes, everywhere. So this way Oh the Web sites that you will visit will have a well automatic security on them so they will automatically generate a yes. Think then you will have another thing that has no script. So that this wait will increase your protection when you navigate on the browser. Next thing we want to do is at the security level. So simply click there. Then we'll go on the security level from here. We're going to talk about all the setup of the tour if you want to set it up as your default browser.

Simply check right here. Once again as I said it's a normal web browser as any other. So you can use it as an everyday project. It's a bit longer because well it's longer because it's more let's say anonymous but you can still visit Google or any other Web site with it all right so here if you want to change the appearance of the tour if you want to change the language is going to be here. Here click the second one because you always want to decide where you will save your files. So let's say you want to save a file on your desktop and then under file at another place.

You can do it or what you can do also is save files too. And then you create another file that you will name Tor and all your files that you downloaded from let's say the deep web. We'll be safe there. But once again don't download files from the Deep Web. But in case you do it then for the updates it's gonna be here. For example if you want to download updates to your tour brother it's gonna be there. So you decide if you want to donate them automatically or if it will ask you to download them. Uh this little thing here is home so it's not very important. It's just to let you decide what is gonna be your homepage so you can add custom if you are ill. Or it could be the page about Tor which is this speech. Same thing for New that next the search. So here you can decide what will be your default search engine.

And finally the security page which is the most important page. First thing you want to click on is right there. So all your cooking data has to be closed when the is closed so you will have no Cookie left on your browser. When the tour browser will be closed, log in the passwords and never leave your passwords anywhere. So your passwords don't have to be saved so don't check those things right here. Once again for history. Always use a private browsing mode. So check this thing there after that for all the permissions. Very simple. You click on settings and you check this box right there so block your requests. This way no one will be able to send your requests if let's say you're on Skype but your I don't know you're doing some face time from the tour browser well you can maybe activate it but when you're browsing the deep web just block all of everyone that can send you a notification to get access to your location camera make or notification.

Same thing here. So check up all the things right there to block websites from automatically being sound pop up windows and the one if a website wants to install add ons. This is for example if the website wants to automatically install something on your computer. Well you will block it there if you want to add some exceptions while you can click there and you add the exception Web site. So this is for example your streaming movies online where you go on the website where there are a lot of pop ups on the surface web.

You can just check this box and you'll have no pop ups on your computer which the rating room then for your security level you have two levels of security standard. This one is when you visit let's say the surf Web lets you use your own google or whatever you take. This one right there. If you want to have a more secure ID you can check a second one will do. It will disable all javascript everywhere but everywhere story on only no no HD s Web sites. So let's say for example it's a dot on your Web site that is not secure. Well it's gonna be disabled.

The javascript will be disabled so you won't see pictures and other things. Same thing for some symbols and well some funds and audio video will be clicked on the click to place. For example we have a video. You will have to click to play videos won't start if you click on them and the last one will. It's the safest one. It's javascript is blocked everywhere so there is no javascript you can't have any attack on your computer. A lot of the icons and symbols and pictures are disabled also. And finally the same thing for audio video and the web. G L Well it's gonna be click to play so if you want to for example watch a video you will have to click on it. Then to check all those tree boxes there it's to block you from dangerous and deceptive content. So you want to check in and the forces that are difficult.

Check the second one. So it's gonna ask every time for the first and for the fifth that right here you have nothing to check it's a bit. Well more advanced features if for example you have a proxy. But for now we don't need to use we don't have to use this feature here so you can see right there. You have Doug Doug. Doug the go which is uh the web browsers with the Twitter browsers search engine. It's a parade. Well it's anonymous, a search engine and that you also have a site where you have a dot onion version of duck duck go for now let's look at what it looks like when you make a search on it. So let's say we look for Duck Duck Go.

The Web version. So as you can see takes a bit more time but you can see it gives you all clear that the results so let's click on the result go. So as you can see it's uh well this is the clear net version of Dr. because it's a dot com Web site but you also have a uh version that is uh for the deep web which is a version that says Dot onion. So let me show you where it looks something like this. So as you can see this Web site is uh well it has a lot of numbers and letters.

It's not a conventional Web site and it's a dot on your Web site. Once again it's just the D version of the good that is done. Well that is on the Deep Web. It's a dot on your Web site. But besides that it's the same dumb that goes on leads as I said a more anonymous version and say it this way. So that's it for the scores guys in you all. In our next class where we are gonna visit some Web sites on the Web.

List Of Safe Websites To Visit

All right so I'll see you in hell guys. And welcome back to another half hour glass about the deep web, the complete introduction in today's class. We are gonna see a list of Websites and even visit some Web sites on the deep web. So how can you access the deep web? The safest way. Um what you can do. Um the first thing that I suggest you guys do is really to access the Haydn week which is like a Web site on the deep web where you have something different.

Well you have different categories and you have other websites so it's a good start. Just start on the deep web. So let's get there. So as you can see the high and key is like a Wikipedia on the s version. Deep in the deep web version. So as you can see you have a lot of categories there. You have. Let's see that there are big volunteer financial services and commercial services and you can find some weird stuff here, for example the gun market. Some also do that stuff. Well it's fun to look at but I don't suggest you visit those places. I mean you have blogs in interesting places.

You have e-mail services on the deep web that can just let you send emails anonymously. You also have social networks as you can see you have a Facebook version of the Deep Web. You have forums. You have a lot of other stuff. Um, so we are going to visit one of the Web sites. Well some of those Websites that are interesting. The first one that I can suggest to you is the SEC mail. So I think it is in the email category. It's this one here. So it looks like this too. It's an e-mail service. Very simply simply sign up you create your uh you only create your email. So once again they don't ask you for your name.

They don't ask you for anything. And that you have an email with them and you can receive emails sent and it's all completely anonymous which is really cool. Um also well as I said you can send emails anonymously. Besides that you have many other things. Also on the deep web I told you guys you have search engine search engines. One of the most popular is torch, so torch is somewhere here who will have torch right there once again you'll see Web sites are loading very slowly as you can see you have a search engine that is torch so we can for example. Well I don't suggest you to. I don't suggest you write down things on search engines but just to do that you have search engines here as uh as you have on the clear web.

Also um you have also the Doug the Google version of the deep web. So we saw it in our previous class. And as I said you have a lot of well different categories. I suggest you just look around. Um what else. Mm mm mm mm mm mm mm mm mm. There are some weird things. For example, you can talk well with random people. It's the thing right here. So it's like a social network where you can talk to one person or you can group chat with random people so let me show you what it looks like. So you said it's like a random chat where people talk with each other. So they said Do you have a lot of weird stuff on the deep web? The majority of it is pretty boring and boring but you can find interesting things.

So as I said guys the first place that you want to visit when you're starting out on the deep web will be really the height and weekend on the height and we will find out all the categories that exist on the deep web we even have Websites that are in other languages. So for example if you want French websites financial Web sites German Web sites you have all this right here. It's a good place to start. What I suggest to you also is to visit some forums or places where you can talk with other people. For example the blogs or forums I suggest you really look at those um you can find interesting information about the deep web as a whole and about the deep web they can suggest you some places and some links. For example if you want books, if you want music.

Well you have all this right here. If I'm not mistaken you have uh well you have books right there. You can just check in. You'll find out that that explains each. Each link has this creature description. Next to it um what else. I think that's it. Um, the same things that you have on the clear on the surface web you have the same versions of this on the deep web and you can do the exact same things on the deep web that you can do on the surface web. The only difference is that on the Deep Web. Well it's all anonymous so you find it a bit more stuff. But besides that it's uh the same thing. And as I said the only difference is that it is anonymous. So that's it for this Book Gates. And see you all in our next class where we're going to talk about tales.

Introduction to TAILS

All right. So once again hello yes and welcome back to another of our Books. I want a complete introduction to the Deep Web. So these glasses we are going to talk principally about tales and well for a tour alternative and we are going to focus on tails. So I'm going to explain exactly what tails are. I'm going to show you the Web site of tails but we are not gonna do the complete setup since this glass is really for.

Once again it's very important for you guys to have an introduction to tales in exactly how it works and what's the difference between tails and that. So let's start all right. So what is tails? So the main difference between tails and tails is that the main difference between tails and tour is first that the tour is like a web browser. Well Tor is a web browser. It's a way for you to connect to the deep web for it. And the other Web site but for tails on the other side it's the complete operating system.

So when you install tails you are literally installing a complete operating system that will help you hide your identity. And it works with Tor. So it helps you. It helps you stay anonymous. So when you install tables that I said you installed tor on tails and you will work with both of them. So you're a nun there really will be the max. Is it better than poor? Well not really because as I said the Tails is really an operating system. Tour is the browser better. It can be good practically. Yes it's better. Why? Because when you are, you are able to use tails anywhere you want. Why? Because well tails is not installed on your computer.

Tails will be installed on the EU is key or it will be installed on a DVD. So this means that you can connect directly to the deep web on any computer that you want without leaving no. Without leaving no trace. So you will leave no trace of that if you use a computer to connect to the web browser. This is why it's cool using this. Well this is still tails also. Well that's why in general tails it is a bit better than tor besides that it's pretty much all the levels of safety there. There is no big difference between them. Tails can be run on Windows Mac on Linux. So it can be run on all types of machines which is also very very cool.

And as I said the main the main quality of tails is that it can run with it can run directly on any computer just with a is key so you make the setup only once you set up your program once and then after that you can run it on any machine that you want or a virtual machine if you guys use a virtual machine. And you know a bit. Well you can run it on the virtual machine as well as on the normal machine. The third thing is it is hard to set up. Well absolutely not. If you guys are interested in setting up tails I suggest you simply follow the steps that they have on their Website. We're going to see it a bit later in this class. So what a look.

Well what the Website looks like and where exactly you need to go to to install your well to install this app if you guys are interested to use it once again this Book is really about using Tor but you can use tails because store it entails also. It's just a system. But no it's not hard to set up at all. It took me. You need some components Of course you need. It takes about two hours of time. You also need eight gigabytes, a way of at least eight gigabytes. But the way they explain it it's very very simple. It's very simple to install can Thales be hacked or compromised.

Yes. If the system that you are using lets say you are using a computer. If the hardware of the computer is compromised while details can be compromised as well and the person that has the computer well can see what you've done on it but if the computer is not compromised and if it's something safe for example let's say you're using a laptop and you want to connect to the deep web from a coffee shop. Well no one's going to notice it because well you're connecting tales whether you are key to your laptop and it's not going to leave no trace that you connected the sales to the laptop. So once again this is why it's amazing to have. And the fact that you can use it to connect to the deep web from any computer is really really an amazing thing to have.

So let's try to find that out on the web so I can show you guys how this software works. One less thing is open source software. So once again it's not going to cost you. I think it's completely free. And once again if you guys want to use it as an alternative to work you can. It's an amazing tool. So let's see what it looks like. So the first thing you want to do is open up your Web browser. Let's say it's Google Chrome. You simply go on Google and you write down tales. So here we go: tails is this program right here. So as you can see you will be on this Web site right. That was in French and you put it in English.

If you want to install it you simply click install. From this point they will ask you where you want to install it. You can install on Windows Mac or Linux simply click on the windows it can have a windows and as you can see they will tell you what exactly you will need for this installation you will need. You will be key to at least eight gigabytes and then it's going to take about one hour. You could take less if your internet speed is faster. But besides that you don't really do anything. You don't need anything more. When the installation is done once again you will need to restart your computer. And from this point there will be.

Why do you step by step how you can install this software directly on your computer while under you will be the key that you will be able to use after that on your computer. So I said Guys , that's an amazing tool. Once again we are not going to go in depth of this tool because we are focusing only on the tour for this class. And then once again it's just an introduction to the deep web, it's not a complete security class. So we are going to stick to it. But if you guys want to go more in-depth and learn a bit more about tells. Well I definitely suggest you to use it because once again it's an amazing way to access the deep web from any type of. So that's it for this class guys. And see you all in our next class.

Introduction To Cryptocurrencies

All right. I'll see you guys. Welcome back to another of our amazing classes about the deep web. The complete introduction in today's class we are going to talk about deep web marketplaces and ways that you will buy products on the Deep Web. The first thing that you guys will need to know is that the deep web or the tour browser everything that is around the deep dark web is made to be and stay anonymous. So the way that you are buying stuff on this kind of market is also made to be and stay anonymous.

This is why you will typically well in ninety nine point ninety nine percent of the time not use your credit card because if a marketplace asks you for a credit card you will definitely be hacked. All your credit card information so never put any of your bank credit card or any information on any deep web marketplaces on those marketplaces you will use an anonymous way of paying for the goods that you were buying. Let's say you are buying a television on the Deep Web. You are going to be anonymous for this television.

How you will pay for it. Well you will bait with cryptocurrency And this is what this Book will be about. We are going to talk about crypto currencies in the next parts as well . In the next classes we're going to talk about how to buy you, how to make purchases and how to navigate that on marketplaces. So let's start as I said, what's a crypto currency? The first thing is that it's an Internet based medium of exchange. What does it mean simply means that it's a way to make purchases on the Internet or in any well, especially on the Internet.

This type of currency became very very popular around the world. It came to life in 2009 with the bitcoin and became very very popular in the years that followed because of its anonymity and the fact that you can't really trace a transaction because once again it's really anonymous and the way that it's made you have public keys you have private keys and all this creates something that adds anonymity to every transaction. Well it gives anonymity to every transaction because you will never have a name, you will never have an address or whatever. And it's really really an anonymous transaction. What brings us to the second point is that it's not controlled by any central authority so how can it stay anonymous?

Well there are no banks that control let's say the bitcoin toward the ETF or any type of crypto currency. And that's an amazing way to keep all transactions well secure. It's like if you were going on let's say on the streets and you buy something cash let's say you were going to someone who's selling ice cream and you buy an ice cream cash. Well no one will know besides the person that sold ice cream that you bought the ice cream cash well that you buy an ice cream. But if you will, let's say you buy this ice cream with a credit card or with a credit card or a debit card.

Well it's going to leave a trace on your bank statement. It's going to say that oh you made this transaction that day. But when you buy with the crypto currency there is no bank statement. There is no well there is nothing it's like paying for something cash to a seller that you don't know and he doesn't know you. So it's really really anonymous and it's really about numbers. You don't know the seller. The seller doesn't know. Don't know you. You transferred the money to him. He transfers the goods to you and there is no middleman. This is the beauty of crypto currency and buying well with the use of crypto currency. This is why as I said it's completely anonymous and there is.

Yeah well there are ways to retrace transactions but once again it's very very hard to trace because it's on the block chain technology. It's not it's not like regular transactions when you have let's say what a credit card you have a bank statement that says Oh that day you went to that store and you bought something in this in this case well in the case of using crypto currencies you have completely complete anonymously because you have no bank statement. Well not only more bank statements you have absolutely no information from where the transaction went and who sent you the goods or whatever it's like illegally like buying something cash from a seller that doesn't know you and you don't know him. So just imagine it that way. All right. So how it works for those who are interested in how crypto currency works.

Once again it's not a crypto currency Of course but just for you guys to understand how it works. Let's say someone requests the transaction via a seller or trade requests a transaction. Let's say you request the transaction from the seller. So after that the request will be well we'll be broke. Yes it would be too cheap to burn the network. That is consistent. That consists of computers and all those computers, let's call them. After that this network will complete the transaction and the block chain technology is how I can explain it. It's really let's say it blocks the way it's built. Imagine blocks one after the other and you can't change let's say one block without changing all the blocks before him. So this creates the security of the transaction.

And that this could not be hacked. Well it's very very difficult to hack a block chain technology since it's a new technology. And once again it's very very hard to retrace all the transactions because of this because as I said it's really well you can see as blocks. But once again it's very complicated to understand. And finally at the end of all this process while the checks transaction is completed usually transactions that involve crypto currency take place. Well , it's almost true there. Well they are made in the second line.

Let's say you make the transaction and it takes one to two seconds to complete the transaction. So once again it's very very secure. And so as I said there is no wealth. There is always a certain risk involved but in our case let's say you are sitting on the light side and you are buying stuff like television or let's say computers or whatever on the deep web. There is no risk for you guys too well to have any problems with crypto currency use.

The only risk that I know it's not really associated with buying or selling stuff is let's say you buy the crypto currency and keep it since it's very very volatile. It's not always a good idea to do. Because once again the price fluctuates a lot and they can go really high the same way that it can go really really low. So you can lose or win a lot of money but once again it's not, it's not a risk that is associated with buying stuff on the deep web.

So right now you know how it works and you know what a crypto currency is. So that completes our Book and c o in our next class where we are gonna talk about how to buy crypto currency and where to find it.

How To Buy Cryptocurrencies

All right. So once again hello guys and welcome back to another of our amazing Books about the deep web, the complete introduction class. We are going to talk about how to buy crypto currency. So right now and so now you know what's the crypto currency. But you need to understand the concept behind buying crypto currency and how to use it. So in the normal world we have money which we can call fight money.

When in a story this money was going to be stored in a bank and we have a bank account then we are able to pay with our card for the crypto currencies which works pretty much the same way. So you take your crypto, you buy your crypto currency and you store it. You have to store it somewhere so you can store it directly on your desktop. But that's not the purpose here. Our goal is to have access to it very very easily. So we are going to use the wallet there. That is direct online so store your crypto currency you will use it well. It could be a wallet.

As I said, it can be stored on your computer directly. It could be a cold storage wallet which is stored on a small server or a small hard drive which is stored somewhere at your home. But once again we are going to talk only about wallets that are online. So off the wall what we are going to talk about today will be Coinbase and block chain dot com. Those two wallets are, I think , very , very useful and very easy to use. We are not going to swell the pictures that you're going to see there are not my account. So it's just an example of how Social accounts are a little bit what it is and how it works and why they are very cool to use.

So the first one that you want to see will be the whole Coinbase. So when you get on the Web site you will have to create yourself an account. So you will have to add your email address and security level. It's security because every time that you want it that you will connect you will receive an asset mass and you will have to enter your code. So it's very very secure. Same thing for block chain. The way it works you get connected when you get connected you will see you will have your watch list here. So you'll have all your coins and the price and how much they cost.

You will be able to buy them. Well when you add a payment method you will be able to buy them. So you can buy what is cool on that coin is that you can buy them you can sell them. It's like really real time. So let's say you buy one bitcoin if the price goes up. Well we can resell it. So you can make money trading, let's say for example you don't go on the darknet and can directly trade your crypto currency on Coinbase which is really really cool. Also when you buy your crypto currency it's going to be stored directly here. So you will be able to see it on your portfolio for the moment as you can see I have no future chances.

And the crypto currencies that you want that you are going to buy the most will be the Bitcoin which is the crypto currency that is the most used on the deep web theorem also. And for the rest well you have more narrow also but once again it really depends on the Web sites that you visit. Let's say a Web site once you get the majority of the Web sites on the deep web will usually use bitcoin. Well let's say another Web site a Web site asks you for a specific cryptocurrency for example do you want to sell your products but only in dash. Well you will be able to come back here and buy your dash cryptocurrency which is once again really really cool because if for example you want to trade your crypto currency you can get traded directly here.

Also if you invite a friend while you get a small commission besides that you have all your prices here. So for all the crypto currencies for the moment they have only 19. As you can see it varies sometimes they add some new crypto currencies sometimes well they did delete some of them so yeah it's really what's cool with the coin is that as I said it's a platform that you can use as a wallet but it's also a trading platform so let's say you're someone who want a trade war who is trading well you can do it directly on Coinbase also if I'm not mistaken those are just the best group of friends is you have a lot more of other crypto currencies here.

Once the end of the crypto currencies that are the most used for like let's say for buying products will be those ones right here. Well the bitcoin and the ETF. And I said maybe Monday or on some websites. But once again it really depends. All right. Next platform will be block chain dot com. So it's absolutely the same way you want to buy yours. Well the first thing you want to do is create your account. So you go on block chain dot com. Once your account is created this platform is really for buying and selling cryptocurrency. So you will have this dashboard right here. So if you want to buy crypto you will just click there you click on buy crypto. They will ask you first. You will not see this thing right there.

You will have to choose your currency so you simply choose your first currency with which you want to buy your crypto. So let's say I'm going to use a British pound. So let's say I want to buy 100 British pounds of crypto currency and as you can see they will connect me here and then we'll have to fill all my personal data and then I can buy my cryptocurrency using a credit card or a PayPal account. Usually it's very very simple, too well to buy crypto. Once you have your crypto currency the way he's going to work you will have a public key and a private key. And when you want to make your transaction normally you will only put on your public key. You will never write down your private key.

And it's very good, it's very simple. Let's say you want to. I don't know if you want to exchange well or you want to send that and send it to someone. So I hear you will write down the public key of the person and you will simply send them your. Well how much you want to send crypto to this person you can send it in money you can send bitcoins. This works the same way when you buy products on the Deep Web. Let's say you choose a product to buy. You will only enter your public key. Normally you don't enter your private key because this one you keep it for you. And yeah so that's it it's very very simple.

Also you can borrow crypto currencies. But once again you need to be at a higher level. So as I said you can buy your crypto currency there. So it's here if you want to swap your crypto currency which is let's say exchange bitcoin for Ethereum it's gonna be there. So you will need to have crypto currency first. We need to buy some. And that's it. Well you can trade also. Once again our goal is really to buy yet crypto is not to trade or whatever. So to buy a crypto currency once again two very very simple platforms use Coinbase block chain they don't require or I don't know how much verifications.

Very simple to use. You enter your name and everything and you can buy your crypto. Once you have your crypto stored there you congratulations you have a wallet with the crypto currency. And from this moment you are able to buy things on the deep web so that's where the scorer's guys right now know exactly how to buy you a crypto currency and where this crypto currency will be stored at this moment. We will see how we can buy your products on the deep web.

Is It Safe To Buy Products On The Deep Web

All right. So once Yes hello Yes And welcome back to another of your amazing Books about the deep web. So in this class we are going to talk about a very interesting subject which is Is it safe to buy things under there. So before we start I'd like to make a quick disclaimer. So everything good that you are going to learn in this class is absolutely educational. So everything is really for education and well you don't really have to do it.

It's just good for education. All right. So when there is, there are two types of what you should know: wait until now you have the surface web and the deep dark web. When you're buying something on the surface web let's say you're buying out on the computer on Amazon. Let's say the computer comes to your place and the computer is not working or the computer just never comes to your place. Well it's very simple for you to call Amazon to explain the problems and you'll receive a complete refund because you have been floated or because the product didn't work. So that's a way that this can work or you can simply call your credit card provider and they will just block the transaction because fraud has happened.

So this is one way that you can do things on the surface with on the Dark Web a bit more. It's a bit more different because everyone is anonymous. Everything that's happening other transactions are the sellers are all the buyers are all anonymous. No one knows who he is dealing with. So the problem here is that if for example you are making a purchase let's say you're buying a television on the Deep Web. Let's say you want to be anonymous and you decide to buy a television on the deep web and the television doesn't work well. Well you don't really have no way to find out the seller or block the transaction or whatever because as they say that you transferred the money to the seller.

Well you will not hear from him after that it's impossible because you can't really find him. You can't really because there is no middleman when you're dealing with crypto currency. It's buyer to seller. So you transfer the money to the seller where the other you're the seller. The buyer transfers you the money you'd transfer him the product but there is no middleman. So in this case you have to trust the seller who is in front of you even if he's anonymous. So now we know that you know all this and you know one of the dangers of dealing with the book. The first thing we are going to talk about here is what it is. If it's safe. But the first way to know if it's safe. Well it's going to be by asking yourself what you are looking for on the deep web.

Everything depends on the type of product that you want. Let's say you want to buy something that exists on the clear web. Let's say you want to buy a television. You're getting on the Web site with it with a lot of I don't know what electronic stuff. And you have one seller that has a lot of reviews and well it's pretty it's very cool. So you buy a television from him. There are more chances that this guy is willing to give good service since he has a lot of reviews since he has a good product. Then the other guy who sells. I don't know which type of product that maybe doesn't have quality in this product and has no reviews or wants to review. So it really works the same way as the surface web but once again it really depends on what you are looking for.

If you're looking for some other type of things. Well I'm not a specialist in those types of things. Once again they said this Book is really for educational purposes. So if you're looking for those types of things for other types of things. Well I can't really help you with that. Second thing where you are looking for it. Once again it's the same with the same thing as on the surface web. When you are buying products from the deep web let's say your main goal is just to remain anonymous. It will depend where you are looking for your products. Let's say once again you want to buy a television on the deep web.

Let's see on the surface what you want to buy this television if you want to buy this television. On the surface web you will go on a Web site that has a certain reputation. So you will go let's say for example on Amazon or you'll go on eBay or on e-commerce. They have a certain reputation of selling good products and that have the traffic and reviews because you want to be sure that you will receive the product. It's the same thing on the deep web. So if you're looking for your television on some random website it's maybe not the place to look for this kind of brother. If you're going instead to a good marketplace that looks good where you see that there is a lot of traffic that people are buying and the product has a lot of use. Well it's may well you have more chances to receive your brother there than from some sketchy Website.

Last thing every Web site on the deep web that asks you for your personal information or your credit card or anything else than a cryptocurrency is. Well you have ninety nine point nine nine percent chances that they tried to just steal your information. So never never never deal with those types of Web sites because the deep web or the dark web are two places where everyone wants to remain anonymous. If a Web site asks you for your credit card in full, ask you for your paypal or whatever type of payment information they ask you for. It's gonna be a scam. So just stay away from those types of Websites. If something is too good to be true. Well it's maybe too good to be true.

Like if you see let's say for example a cell phone for the equivalent of one hundred dollars an iPhone X for the equivalent of one hundred dollars in bitcoins on some Web site. Well it's probably a scam. So be very very careful with those types of things. So as I said guys the first thing we want to identify is what you're looking for and what you want to buy. Once again if you're looking for electronic stuff, there are some things that exist on the surface web and you want to buy them simply anonymously on the Deep Web.

It's possible there are marketplaces for this. Then you want to find those marketplaces. We will look at some of them in our next class. And finally never use Web sites that use anything else than cryptocurrency. Because those Websites only try to steal your information and you will not remain anonymous. So there is no point in using those types of Web sites because in the end you could just buy your product on the surface web. So that's it for this Book guys. See you all in our next class.

Market Places

All right. Once again Hello guys and welcome back to another of our Books about the deep web. This class we are going to talk about marketplaces and how to buy stuff on the deep web. So in India what's the dark web? It's very hard to find products when you want to buy some products right there. Why? Because well you want to find the people that are trustful. You want to find Web sites that are trustful.

And I personally don't buy things on the dark web because I just go there to read for example news or just to read books. This is my main purpose. But we are going to look at some marketplace and what they are looking like. And once again this Book is really for you guys to see what. Well what type of things you can find on the Deep Web. And it's really for educational purposes more than buying real products from the Deep Web. Well if you want to buy some legal products that's OK. But once again this for that's for you is just for educational purposes. So that's the first thing that we want to do is go on our site and we keep a Web site so you can simply copy the U or L that you see here directly on your computer from this point when you write it down you can simply click on enter.

You should be back on the Web site right here so you have a lot of luck. Always have a lot of things. And then we are going to look at commercial services and marketplaces there. So we are going to look at commercial services. There are other height and weekly Web sites that exist well; they have plenty of those that exist. This one is my favorite because you only have good links on it but you have some other Websites that exist. For example this one also says it's in like the height and we keep because you have. Well you have here the links and you have the what. Well those are the descriptions of the link. What you can find. So for example doors.

Well it's a search engine marketplace for example right here. You have. OK. You have nail growers. It's a coffee shop. Great. Can. So as you can see you have a lot of interesting things here too. Once again that's another type of high. And we Keats just links and well you have the description of the link. Let's go back to our Heidi with you right here. So we want to let's say we want to look for products for example and buy some electronics for example cell phones or computers. So we will look at commercial services. OK. What we have here is the first link to mobile stores. So it effectively unlocked the iPhone and other smartphones.

We'll look at this Web site right there and what we have. Okay. Do we have something else like Apple for bitcoins? We have another Web site that sells cheap Apple products for bitcoins. All right. So we have two Websites that will visit all right. So the first one is this one. So it's a Web site that sells iPhones. So as you can see, the iPhone X is 256 gigabytes and is sold for this price and you will pay one bit in bitcoins. So it's always in Bitcoins that you pay on the deed on the dark web. As I said if the price were in USD and they told you to put on your credit card well once again it would be a complete scam. Well as you can see you have here the price and it was the end. It's converted into bitcoins. Same thing here. So if you want to buy a Samsung Galaxy stand well you have your price in you're price in bitcoins. So you simply click to choose your country equally or you click on buy now and you will have to create yourself an account.

Once again when you create an account you only enter a user name password. You don't have to enter a new address no nothing. You simply enter username and password. And when you will have filled everything that's from this well when you will buy your product it's only there that you will enter your address. So let's look at the second Web site OK. It looks about the same as an iPhone , sorry. So once again you have an iPhone brother right here as you can see they are sold for three hundred thirty five USD or 400. Were these usually just products either are they directly sold from the manufacturer for example. You have an employee of the business that is working in some other country and well they have the product for less or I don't know how to get the product but at the end of the day.

Well you can have it at this price. But once again I personally never bought a product on the Deep Web site's dark web. I can't really recommend this because this Of course is really about initiating you to the dark web not really buying products. So if you want to do it that's up to you. But once again just to show you how it works. Same thing for MacBook Pros as you can see here you have a MacBook pros at this price. So we'll never find this type of price on the surface. I work the exact same way, let's say, when I buy an iPhone. Simply click on buy now.

Once again we do. Yes. Sometimes it's gone. It takes time. OK so you get the point. It takes a little bit too much time. But OK.

So once again as you can see they ask you to log in. So you have to log in or create a new account to be able to make the best transaction. So he works the exact same way you will simply have to create yourself an account. And at the end only you will enter your address well the address where you want to send the brother to for example you want to buy this product.

Well if you want to send it somewhere that's where you can enter your address is what is the exact same way as buying products on the surface web only you can have it for way cheaper here. Once again it's not always sure that the Web site is legit or the seller is legit and that you will have received the product. So you will have to be very very careful about this. So as I told you guys the first thing you want to do is really go on our hide and we do Web sites. You go to marketplaces. And right here you can have a lot of different marketplaces that are very interesting. So if you want to buy, I don't know if you want to buy iPhones or other products.

Well everything is there. You also have some other alternatives right here or this one you can just copy the link that you see here on your computer and from there you will have access to plenty of links and all those links. Well ah well you have some marketplaces and all those links and well you can simply go and take a look at marketplaces. But once again I really suggest you just take a look. I don't know if you want to see what it looks like or just for fun but besides that. Well it's just a deep web so if you want to take a look at it just for fun I really see.

Well I suggest you find interesting things. But once again I don't really suggest people to buy things on those marketplaces if you want to do it. Once again it's up to you. But I don't suggest it. So that's it for the scores guys right now. You know how to access marketplaces and what type of products you can find here. If you want to visit by yourself, well that's up to you. It's going to increase your experience in visiting the dikes, the deep, large dark web. Besides that, that's where this test can see you all in our next class.

The Dangers Of The Dark Net

All right so once again Hello and welcome back to another of our Books about the deep web. In today's class we are going to talk about all the dangers that are present on the darknet. So yeah let's start. So the first thing before looking at all those points of the darknet as you saw in various classes is a world of a lot of things you can have very interesting things such as libraries or all kinds of stuff where you can look at them all on your.

We can hide and we can. But also you can find a lot of other types of things that are not as amazing as they are. This is why it could be also one of for me honestly I consider this as one of the biggest dangers of the deep web because it can. Well when you see certain stuff sometimes it's not you don't really want to see them. So we can see it that way. This is one of the dangers of the Deep Web. But from a technical point of view. First of all you have a lot of viruses and malware in a lot of Websites. So if you visit a bad Web site, sometimes you can have viruses or malware or a lot of stuff like this. So it's very very very important for you guys to be very careful on the Web site that you are visiting.

Once again this Book is really just an introduction so just introductions show you what exists. Show you what to do and what not to do. It's not a complete Book of both security where you wake up playing you how to hide everything and all this kind of stuff. So it's really just an introduction. So just try to stay away from certain kinds of Web sites and if you don't know a Website link well simply just don't click on it. If you are sure about a link or a Web site will begin going visit it's the same thing as the surface web. Just you have to be a bit more cheerful because once again there is no sin censor on the Deep Web.

You can find a lot of disturbing things sometimes. And those disturbing things can come with the mail whereas in viruses also and the type of viruses that you have on the deep web can sometimes be very very powerful and just destroy your computer. So worth it to steal all your banking information. So be very very careful about this. Never click on the link quote that you don't know. Second thing users can find where you are once again it's not all users I'm talking about. Some good hackers. So if there are some Websites on the deep web and there are some stories of people who have been tracked down because they insulted some other people or they just acted badly with some people. So be very careful.

Once again I'm saying this. It's not that you are anonymous on the Deep Web. Don't worry, everything's anonymous. We've signed up for this Book. If you're using Thales and Tor you should be anonymous but once again you don't want to offend the wrong person because you have good people on the deep web but you also have a lot of criminals. So you have to be careful with the people that you are dealing with. So from this point of view try to be very very careful. So this can be also one of the dangers of the deep well the dark web on the deep web of the dark web. And it's not the last thing. It's not the deep slash dark web that is dangerous in itself as a whole because what it is in the end is just a lot of websites put together. It's the people they can beat on it.

It's like the surface web. But on the deep web since there is a lot of a lot more criminality that is going on in this place. Well the Dark Web is more dangerous. So there are more dangerous people in this type of place. So try to not give your reserve banking information to those people because once again if you start doing so well guess what's going to happen if you are often the wrong person and they have your information. Well you don't know what they can do. So those are for me the dangers of the dark web.

The biggest one as I said is often viruses and mailers to others. Yes they are here. But if you act simply as a normal person well you should not happen to you but be very careful about viruses and malware so just the websites that you are visiting trade not visit all the links that you see because once again there is no censors on the Web. On the Deep Web site the dark web. So you need to be sure about the Websites that you guys are visiting. So that's it for this Book guys and see you all in our next class.

Staying Safe

Rights holders and welcome votes on other far Books in today's class. We are going to talk about some tricks that you can use to stay safe on the Deep Web so you are going to see the trades. I'm going to give you a very simple one. We talked about them in our other classes. It's absolutely the same thing that you can use on the surface web honestly. So the first one would be not clicking on the links. So for you guys most of you will be beginners when you go on the forum because that's one of the things that everybody will do when they start out on the Deep Web.

They go on forums, they go on different social networks and you'll see there are a lot of people that will post links. The last thing that you guys want to do is click on those links because it's well you never know where those links can take you. So once again the first thing you want to do is never click on links. You can start out your deep web journey as we saw by going on Hyden wiki which is an amazing place. You have links, those links for the majority of them are just as sure. Well they're very well, they're safe for the majority of them. So those are things that you can use. You can find out other things.

The more you're going to be on the deep web the more you get to meet people. Well you get to know more places. Once again just don't start clicking on every link that you find on the deep web because it's going to end up very badly for your computer. Second thing, don't visit sites that you don't know. It's exactly the same thing as we talked about. The first one will not click on links to the third thing. Don't trust people on forums. So the majority of forums while once again you have forums where they talk about ethical hacking. You have a forum where it's more trustworthy. But in the majority of forums people don't trust people everywhere. It's like it's the same thing as on the surface web. If you start trusting everyone that tells you I can make you one million dollars.

Well guess what you're going to get scammed. So we don't trust people on forums and don't follow no one on those forums. You can go there to try to learn new stuff but if people start to put links in this kind of stuff don't click on them besides that on your tour browser stay on the safest level. So when you're browsing on the darknet stay on the safe on the safest level because you won't. You don't want no one to get access to your computer and not only this when you're sitting on the surface level. Well you can be. People will not attack you with phishing attacks and also pictures will not show up. So you'll stay really really safe from absolutely everything. And the last thing. Do not enter information.

And for me your information's anywhere. So once again that's the most important of all: your information is very precious, your bank information, your Social number or all this type of information. Don't put it anywhere even if you think you found a job somewhere on the Deep Web. Well don't put your information because once again that's the best way for them to just hack your information and sell your identity on some other Web site that resells identities. So once again guys stay safe for the rest. As we saw in our first classes how to set up our tour browser. So set it up on the max level of safety. Not only this.

Don't forget to check all the buttons on your tour browser. As we saw in the first Book. So this way no one will exit your camera on your monitor and well nothing. And you don't want to let no one. Don't go on the social web sites on the deep web where you can facetime with people who were taught by camera with people because once again you never know with whom you're going to talk. And those Web sites are in the majority of times not secure. And it's just a way for you guys to just steal money from you or just hack your computer. So that's it for this Book guys. And see you all in our next class where we are going to talk about the Book summary.

Conclusion

All right. Once again Hello guys. Welcome back to our last last about the deep web, the complete introduction so congratulations guys you completed the whole Book. So until now what you saw you know exactly you should know exactly what is the deep web. So that's what we saw at the beginning of the Book. You shouldn't know the difference between the deep web and the dark web. Because yes there is an important difference between both of them.

Also you know how we can be used for legal purposes and that right now you should know also that the Dark Web is not only a place where everyone is evil and only bad people will be there. You have very good people that go there only for news to be able to access Web sites. There are censors in their countries to be able to access news that is censored in their countries. And once again this is a good thing for you guys to know because if you're living in some countries where information is censored. Well you can access it. You can use it in our browser to access this information about the third browser.

After that we had a complete introduction about it. So right now you should know what the third browser is, how it works, and how to set it up. We talked about this to our security, what's the security of Tor and seek some safety tricks. After I talked about the concept of anonymity and why people wanted to be anonymous when they visit when they go on the Internet. The difference between the surface web and the dark web also like people who are anonymous why exactly they don't care to be anonymous on the surface women on the deep web they want to be anonymous. Everywhere we went on the life part we downloaded the tor browser. So right now you should have the tour browser on your computer. You should be able to access it well because it's on your computer.

And also you should be able to access the height in which you are right now because it's the place where you want to be where you will be able to find all of your links to all the deep web web sites which is a really good thing to start in this field. Also you should know right now about tales. We had an introduction about tales so once again we didn't have a practical comp. We didn't have a practical Book about tales because once again my goal here was only to make a complete introduction and talk more about the Book about the deep web in theory than create a complete security class where I'm going to talk how to set up tales have and how to set up everything it was just an introduction just for the purpose of you guys to know that this exists.

So once again as I said we talked about tales and I really recommend you guys to get this program because once again it's a free software and you can use it toward browsers. And once again Tales is really an operating system so you can use it with the tor browser you can put tor on it and use it that way and you will be able to use them on all kinds of computers. So once again I hope you guys will use it. Next thing we saw how to make purchases on the Deep Web. We had an introduction about cryptocurrency. We talked about crypto.

We had a practical Book on the How to Buy crypto, how to get access to how to have a crypto wallet, and we saw if it's safe to buy products on the Web. We sell some market policies on life. Finally we talked about the dangers of the darknet and how to stay safe. And right now you guys have completed and you have all this information. I hope you guys will use it the right way. Once again all this was only for a decisional purpose. You guys right now know that all this exists. Of course we can visit the deep web and it's not illegal at all to visit it. I highly recommend you guys to visit it. It's for reading books and fighting going on the deep web library for example.

We're going to go on forums reading about different subjects because there are a lot of things that are censored on the normal web on the surface web that are not censored on the deep web. So this is why I highly recommend you guys to take a look at it but don't forget to stay very very careful because once again this is. It could be. Well there is no censor. So if there is no censor, you can find any kind of information. This is why I'm asking you guys to stay safe and that you don't get into antivirus and using tales you can use only Tory can work. It will protect your anonymity buddy if you want to be able to use it anywhere, for example any computer.

Well I really suggest you to download Toure instead of downloading tales sorry instead of just downloading Toure on all computers that you find besides that forget the eyes this Book is really for educational purpose the deep web can be very very dangerous. But right now that you have all this information I hope you guys like the Book and what's the end it was just a complete introduction.

It wasn't supposed to go really in-depth or do some expert things like going in and seeing all the security around this. This is just an introduction gate for you to be able to get access to the Deep Web. And for you guys to know a little bit how all this works. So that's it for this Book guys. And see you in any other of my Books at another time. So thanks again and see you.